LIFE IN THE SPIRIT

A Biblical View of the Person & Work of the Holy Spirit in Melanesian context

An Inductive Bible Study for groups and individuals

by Pastor Dole Peter

Life in the Spirit
A Biblical View of the Person and Work of the Holy Spirit in Melanesian context

Copyright © 2019 Dole Peter

This book or parts thereof may not be reproduced in any form, stored in a retrieval system, or transmitted in any form - electronic, mechanical, photocopy, recording or otherwise - without prior permission of the publisher. Permission is granted for up to 10 copies of a single study when used for group study purposes.

Published by NENGE BOOKS, Australia
ABN 26809396184
nengebooks1@gmail.com
www.nengebooks.com

Concept, design, layout & editing - Nenge Books
Cover photo - Storm clouds over the Aramia River near Kawito, WP, PNG .
Photo copyright © 2019 Michael Jelliffe.

Updated May 2024

This book is available for churches at wholesale prices direct from Nenge Books.
Order from nengebooks1@gmail.com

ISBN 978-0-6484284-2-8

CONTENTS

Introduction 5
Acknowledgements 6
Study 1 - Why are People Confused? 7
    The Three Houses 7
Study 2 - The Blessings & Battles of the Christian Life ... 14
Study 3 - The Holy Spirit and the Work of the Church 18
    Understanding the Holy Spirit 18
    Who is the Holy Spirit? 20
Study 4 - The Ministry & the Gifts of the Holy Spirit 24
Study 5 - The Message of the Holy Spirit 29
Study 6 - Recognising and dealing with the Enemy of the Holy Spirit 36
Study 7 - The Fruit of a False Spirit 43
Study 8 - Testing the Spirits 47
    Tests to see if it is the work of the Holy Spirit 48
Bibliography 52

How to use this study

To use this study, read the Bible verse and then answer the question being asked with the best answer you can give, as an individual or as a group.

Key:

📖 Indicates a Bible passage to read.

✍ Indicates a question which requires a response from you. This may be your individual written response or a group discussion.

The foundation material for this book originated in a study by a group of Evangelical Church of PNG pastors and students at the Christian Training Centre, Mapoda, WP. The material was rewritten into the format used in this book as an inductive Bible study by Pastor Dole Peter.

INTRODUCTION

My purpose in writing this study book is so that a clear understanding of the ministry of the Holy Spirit is basically known very well to every believer living in the time of revival. One needs to know the work of the Holy Spirit and appreciate him. Likewise it is necessary to know about the person of the Holy Spirit in order to accept fully the word of the Holy Spirit.

A study of the Spirit's personality and deity in different ways may seem not very interesting to some, but knowing who the Holy Spirit is and what he does, both His person and work, is both basic and vital to Christian devotion and living.

People look for different things during a time of revival and are confused by which Spirit to follow. There can be nothing new or anything more added to that which Jesus had already promised in John 14:15 – 31. For He has already given us His Holy Spirit to live within us. But most Christians look for new miracles, the secret things, and are completely overlooking the freely given gift the Holy Spirit.

The Holy Spirit is freely given to us and wants to overflow in our lives. We desperately need to know more of Him. With increased knowledge will come added faith, power and control in our lives.

ACKNOWLEDGEMENTS

Once again I thank God, the Father, Son Jesus Christ and Holy Spirit. My wife Sulamato is my greatest blessing, my comforter and my shield through all of life's challenges as we both shared questions to put into this study book. My two big kids Doris and Walter also contributed their input thoughts.

My writing collaborator and dear Spiritual brother in Christ and key person Mike Jelliffe again helped me to rearrange this material well for which I am grateful. Mike I want to salute you for your hard work as you wanted Melanesian Christians to write books in their own context. Your feedback inspires me and letters sustain me.

Also my deepest thanks to Nenge Books publishing in Australia for publishing this from first draft.

Ps Dole Peter
Rumginae

STUDY 1 - WHY ARE PEOPLE CONFUSED

The Three Houses.

HOUSE 1

📖 Read 1 Timothy 1:3-4

Paul, who wrote this letter to Timothy, asks him to do three things. What are those three things?

✎ 1. (vs 3) Stay in Ephesus.

✎ 2. (vs 3) Command certain men not to teach false doctrines.

✎ 3. (vs 4) Command certain men ... not to devote themselves to endless myths and genealogies.

'Myth' is defined as "a traditional story, especially one concerning the early history of a people or explaining a natural or social phenomenon, and typically involving supernatural beings or events."

Do you have traditional stories that describe supernatural beings or events in your culture?
✎

If so, describe one story you know about?
✎

'Genealogy' is defined by the dictionary as "a line of descent traced continuously from an ancestor".

Is genealogy important in your culture? Why?

✎

Does your genealogy extend to ancestors in the spiritual realm? If so, explain how.

✎

If Paul was writing to your church, what do you think he would mean by telling people 'not to devote themselves to endless myths and genealogies'?

✎

Do you think some Christians are confused because they are trying to hold on to both their Christian beliefs and traditional beliefs, especially about ancestor spirits? Why do you think they are confused?

✎

Are some people still living in fear of ancestoral spirits? How do you know?

✎

Read Titus 3:9

What do you think Paul means when he asks Timothy to "avoid foolish controversies and genealogies and arguments and quarrels about the law, because these are unprofitable and useless"?

House 1 represents Christians who are living in fear and confusion because they are trying to hold onto traditional beliefs about the spirits and Christianity. We want to follow Christ and have him like a roof over our heads to protect us 'if anything happens to us', but we also believe in the things our ancestors taught us.

What can we do to resolve this confusion?

✍

This house shows us that our lives are sometimes a mixture of our traditional beliefs and our new beliefs about Christ and the Christian way of life.

Example: A PNG person visiting overseas returned to PNG and told family members that he had seen his mother there. The mother had died several years before that.

How was he influenced by traditional explanations of death?

✍

HOUSE 2

 Read Deuteronomy 18:9-11.

Vs 9: What instructions did the Lord give to the Israelites as they prepared to enter the Promised Land?

✍

Vs 10-11: List the 'detestable ways' that God specifically mentions.

✎

How important is spiritual power in your culture? Do people easily follow someone who is recognised as having supernatural power? Can you give an example?

✎

Do you think some people actually seek spiritual power from the spirits? Can you give an example?

✎

📖 **Read 1 Corinthians 1:22 and Matthew 16:1**

What were the Jews looking for?

✎

Are people today also looking for signs (such as miracles, healing etc) and special spiritual experiences? Give an example.

✎

In House 2 we mix different beliefs about supernatural things, like submarines, angels, superhuman powers, divination, special healing powers, and power that comes from other spirits, with Christ and the Holy Spirit and God's Word.

We want to believe in both powers to get special power for ourselves. Again we are confused and live in fear of what could happen.

Example: Some years ago a pastor gave a bottle of secret liquid to another pastor and told him to put the liquid on his skin before preaching to be powerful as a preacher. The pastor followed his instructions and put the liquid on his skin over a period of time. However he later experienced severe skin problems where his skin shrivelled up and he could not even see properly. He called for medical help and was prescribed some medicine to put on his skin. In a day he had recovered. The pastor also felt that the liquid did not do anything to improve his preaching and threw the liquid away.

How does this true story indicate that the pastor was looking for extra spiritual power?

HOUSE 3

 Read Romans 6:6-14.
(vs 6) Paul talks about our 'old self'. What does he mean?

What does Paul say has happened to our 'old self' once we believe in Christ?

(vs12-13) What should we be doing with our body as Christians? How can we do this in our culture?

 Read Galatians 5:16-18
(vs 17) How does living by the Spirit of God relate to our sinful nature? What is the result on our lives?

(vs 16) How can we overcome our sinful nature?
✍

As Christians we should put to death the old beliefs and the strange beliefs, and trust God and His Word fully.

We are under the cover of Christ's blood because He died, rose again and went up to heaven to save us from our sins. The only power we need is the power of his Holy Spirit. We are controlled by Him.

 Read John 8:31-32

What does Jesus say happens when we are his disciples?
✍

Do you think this freedom includes release from traditional spiritual beliefs?
✍

 Read John 16:13-15

Why does Jesus call the Holy Spirit "the Spirit of Truth"?
✍

How will the Spirit of Truth act? How will he relate to Jesus?
✍

Why do we need any other spiritual power?
✍

📖 **Read John 15:26**

What name and role does the Holy Spirit have according to these words of Jesus?

✍

📖 **Read John 17:17**

How does Jesus describe the Word of God?

✍

📖 **Read John 14:6**

How does Jesus describe himself?

✍

What does Jesus say about different ways to gain spiritual power to get to the Father?

✍

📖 **Read Acts 4:12**

How many ways are there to gain salvation? Are there other means of gaining salvation?

✍

REFLECTION

We should not be confused or frightened. We should have confidence in God the Father, God the Son, God the Holy Spirit, and the Word of God as Truth.

STUDY 2 - THE BLESSINGS AND BATTLES OF THE CHRISTIAN LIFE

In Study 1 we have seen the three houses where most Christians are confused about their beliefs and assurance in God.

Now let us look into some of the things which God has promised us and some things He has warned us will happen.

When they turn to Christ, people experience changes in their lives, there is an outpouring of revival in the church, God is at work in the lives of Christians and people are touched in a special way. We see that when God is at work, Satan is also at work to spoil the work of God.

Read these verses very carefully to find what God has promised, and what God has warned of.

What has God promised?	What has God warned?
Matthew 28:20	John 16:33
Acts 2:17-21	2 Timothy 3:1-5
John 16:13	1 Timothy 4:1-5
John 10:28,29	1 Peter 5:8

Every believer should test new spiritual experiences.

 Read 1 John 4:1
What kind of spirit do we need to believe? What are we told to do?

Warnings about False Teaching and the Spirits

Christians can be tricked if they do not test everything by the Bible. What do these verses say about false Christs?
 Matthew 7:21-23; Matthew 24:23-25

 Read Romans 16:17-18
vs 17 What are the two tactics Paul urges these brothers to watch for?
 1.

 2.

Vs 18 Who are these people serving and how do they deceive?

Do you see people like this in your own culture or community?

📖 Read 2 Corinthians 11:13-14
Who is behind these people?
✍

📖 Read 2 John 1:7-8
What two names does John give to false teachers? What is their relationship to Jesus Christ?
✍

What kind of believers will be fully rewarded?
✍

Sometimes Satan may use believers.
📖 Read Matthew 16:23
How did Satan use Peter?
✍

Why did Jesus rebuke Peter?
✍

📖 Read Acts 8:9-24
Are there believers who practice magic in the church today?
✍

How do they behave in their Christian lives?

✍

It is good to test every spirit to see if it is a deceiving spirit from Satan, or from God.

📖 Read 1 Thessalonians 5:21-22
What are we to hold on to, and what are we to avoid?

✍

All believers are told to test the spirits.

REFLECTION

Jesus won a great victory when He died on the cross, rose from the dead and now sits at the right hand of God. He has defeated Satan who has no power to hold him in the tomb. This power of Jesus is available to us through the Holy Spirit.

STUDY 3 - THE HOLY SPIRIT AND THE WORK OF THE CHURCH

Study 2 has shown us clearly that Satan is at work and is trying to spoil the lives of Christians and the church too.
Therefore now as Christians we all need to know who the Holy Spirit is and how he works.

Understanding the Holy Spirit

In my culture what is our view about the Holy Spirit?
✎

What kind of spirits were my ancestors worshipping?
✎

What did they do to the people?
✎

LIFE IN THE SPIRIT

The truth of who the Holy Spirit is, is of fundamental importance. To deny Him is to deny His real existence, the existence of the Trinity and the teaching of the Bible.

📖 Read 1 Corinthians 2:10-11, Isaiah 11:2, Ephesians 1:17
What human-like characteristics does the Holy Spirit have?
✍

📖 Read Romans 8:27; 1 John 2:1
What does the Holy Spirit do according to these verses?
✍

📖 Read 1 Corinthians 2:13
What does this verse teach us and what is the Holy Spirit's work?
✍

📖 Read Ephesians 4:30
How does the holy Spirit feel when a believer engages in sinful actions?
✍

In summary -
- The Holy Spirit is a personality.
- The Holy Spirit knows and searches the things of God.
- The Holy Spirit is said to possess a mind.
- The Holy Spirit has an intellect and is able to teach people.
- The Holy Spirit has emotion.
- The Holy Spirit prays on our behalf.

Who is the Holy Spirit?

What do these verses tell us about the Holy Spirit?

📖 Genesis 1:1-3
✍

📖 Genesis 1:26
✍

📖 Numbers 11:25
✍

📖 John 20:21-25
✍

📖 Read Acts 2:1-4

What was happening when the Holy Spirit was given at Pentecost?
✍

What was happening to the believers?
✍

Is it the same today when the Holy Spirit visits the church?
✍

LIFE IN THE SPIRIT

There were lots of new experiences when the Holy Spirit came on the day of Pentecost.

📖 Read Acts 1:5, 2:4, 17

Can we expect the same kind of experiences that the early church had?

✎

If you answer No, then what can we expect?

✎

Read these verses and list some of the experiences that the early believers had during and following Pentecost:

Verses	Experiences
a. Acts 2:3-4	
b. Acts 2:38	
c. Acts 2:41	
d. Acts 2:42 (a)	
e. Acts 2:42 (b)	
f. Acts 2:42 (c)	
g. Acts 2:46 (a)	
h. Acts 2:46 (b)	
i. Acts 2:47	

LIFE IN THE SPIRIT
The Holy Spirit is a gift to each Believer

📖 Read Acts 1:4; Luke 24:48-49; John 16:7-15
Who promised to give the Holy Spirit to the disciples?
✎

📖 Read John 15:26; 16:13-14
Why was the Holy Spirit given to the disciples?
✎

📖 Read Acts 2:38-39; Acts 8:19-20
What do we have to do to receive the Holy Spirit?
✎

Can we get God's gift any other way?
✎

📖 Read John 1:12-13
When we believe in Jesus, what is our new relationship with God?
✎

📖 Read Galations 4:6; Romans 8:9
Where does God send His Holy Spirit?
✎

📖 Read Romans 8:9-11
Can someone be a Christian without the Holy Spirit?
✎

📖 Read Acts 1:8
What would happen when the Holy Spirit was given?
✍

📖 Read John 16:14
Who is honoured by the Holy Spirit?
✍

The Holy Spirit is given to the Church

The church was a recognised group of people, like it is today.

📖 Read Acts 2:2-4, 10:44-48; 15:7-9
To which two groups of people was the Holy Spirit given as part of the body of the church?
✍

REFLECTION

The Holy Spirit was given to people who repented and believed in Jesus, accepting His sacrificial death on the cross for the forgiveness of sins. The Holy Spirit enters our life at conversion and leads us in our personal relationship with God through Christ.

In the next study we consider how the Holy Spirit empowers the church for ministry through His gifts, working together in the building of God's Kingdom on earth.

Looking at the list of the first experiences of the early believers in Acts 2, what can we say to the Church today, is it the same or not? (refer to the discussion on page 21)
✍

STUDY 4 - THE MINISTRY AND THE GIFTS OF THE HOLY SPIRIT

There is only one true Holy Spirit who is from God and He gives gifts for ministry in the church today. However there are many people who are confused about the work of the Holy Spirit within the church.

Read Ephesians 4:12-13

Vs 12 What is the work of the Holy Spirit in the church?

In verses 13: What are the three goals given by the Holy Spirit for the church for?

1.

2.

3.

Read John 14:16

The Holy Spirit is also called what?

What will the Counsellor do in these verses?

John 14:16-17

John 14:26
✎

John 16:7-11
✎

John 15:26
✎

John 16:13-15
✎

The Gifts of the Holy Spirit

📖 Read Ephesians 4:11
What are the five gifts listed in verse 11?
✎
1.

2.

3.

4.

5.

Do we have people with these gifts in the church today?
✎

📖 Read Romans 12:6-8
List the gifts below:
✍

What of these gifts are exercised today in the church?
✍

📖 Read 1 Corinthians 12:7-11
List the gifts of the Holy Spirit stated in this passage:
✍

Why are these different gifts given to different people?
✍

To whom are they given?
✍

The place of the Holy Spirit's Gifts in the church today

Here are some questions that need to be asked.
What gifts of the Holy Spirit do people have today?
✍

Should we ask for those gifts and use them in our worship?
✍

How can people use the gifts they have now?
✍

What are some of the gifts not used and why are they not used?
✍

REFLECTION

When the gifts are given and are used in the local church and church worship, we need to be very careful in how they are used. The word used for spiritual gifts in the Greek text is "charismata", from the word "charis" which means "grace". They are not something we can buy or earn, they are given to us by God as his gifts of grace, to build up the church.

Are the gifts used for God's glory to help the church or are people using them to make a name for themselves?

We need to think very carefully that the gifts are given to glorify God not ourselves, given also for the building of God's kingdom here on earth.

STUDY 5 - THE MESSAGE OF THE HOLY SPIRIT

We have seen in the previous studies that the Holy Spirit is a person, who can communicate with people. So there was a message given to the church on the day of Pentecost.

📖 Read Acts 1:4
What did the Lord promise to send?
✍

Where were they when the promise came true?
✍

The Time when the Holy Spirit came down.

📖 Read Acts 2:14-36
Vs 15. What was the time of the day?
✍

📖 Read Acts 2:1, Acts 4:31
When the Holy Spirit came what is the message (which is found in the book of Acts 2:1-47) given to the early church?
✍

In our culture when there is news of joy people gather together and start telling what they have experienced. There will be lots of laughter and smiles as they express how they feel about the event that has happened during the day.

Peter's message to the Jews during Pentecost.

📖 Acts 2:14-15

Why was Peter trying to explain what was happening to the people who were in Jerusalem?

✍

How do people react when they are filled with the Holy Spirit?

✍

📖 Acts 2:16 Who is the prophet Joel?

✍

📖 Acts 2:17-21 What are the messages of prophet Joel?

✍

Has the message come true in our modern lifetime?

✍

📖 Acts 2:22-24

The purpose of God was beyond the reasoning of a human view point. Why was God's purpose fulfilled by Jesus when He suffered the most pain from wicked men?

✍

How much have you suffered for righteousness? How would you explain this?

✍

📖 Acts 2:25-30

What is Peter saying about David in these verses?

✍

About the Lord? Vs 25

✍

Expression of joy? Vs 26

✍

About the grave? Vs 27

✍

About the life? Vs 28

✍

Vs 29 Where is David's tomb?

✍

LIFE IN THE SPIRIT

Vs 30 Who is the one of the descendants that God promised to be on the throne that Peter is talking about?

✍

Vs 31-36

These verses show the power of God.
What does it say about the power of death?

✍

About the power of resurrection?

✍

About power of Jesus' ascension to Heaven?

✍

About Christ glorified?

✍

vs 38-37-47

It shows the results of Pentecost and warns of the need to repent and have sins forgiven.

Vs 37 What happened to the people after hearing the message?

✍

In this verse what was the result of their repentance from their sins?

✍

What can we see in today's church in PNG especially when people put things right with others and ask for forgiveness?

✍

Peter's message to the Gentiles at the house of Cornelius.

 Read Acts 10:1-48

The importance of this event records the ministry of Peter which will continue with the ministry of the apostle Paul. Although Paul is the apostle to the Gentiles, it is Peter who opened the door to the Gentiles by entering the house of Cornelius and presenting salvation through Christ to his household.

The Jews defined people broadly into two main categories, Jew and non-Jew, or Gentile. To be recogised as a Jew, one had to be born a Jew, or be a converted to Judaism, including undergoing circumcision. Within the Gentiles some were recognised as being "God-fearers", people who exhibited Godly characters and a heart for God but had not converted to Judaism. The rest were regarded as "pagans".

Vs 1 Who was Cornelius?

✍

Vs 2 What kind of people were he and his family? What two things did they do to demonstrate their spirituality?

✍

LIFE IN THE SPIRIT

📖 Acts 10:34-36

What does this verses say about God's act of choosing?
✍

📖 Acts 10:38

How did God anoint Jesus and what was his job on earth?
✍

vs 39 Has Jesus been crucified as part of God's plan?
✍

vs 40-41 What happened to Jesus when he was in the tomb?
✍

vs 42 God appointed Jesus as who? And what will he do?
✍

vs 43 What was the message that Peter preached?

vs 44-46 What happened to the Gentiles who heard the message?
✍

vs 47-48 What was Peter's response to witnessing the Gentiles receiving the gift of the Holy Spirit?

Compare the messages that Peter spoke during the time of Pentecost and the message to the household of Cornelius? Are they similar or not? How do they vary?

 Acts 15:5-11

There was oppositon from some Jewish Christians who believed that Gentile Christian converts should still be circumcised (ie. obey Jewish law). How does Peter refute them during the church Council at Jerusalem? What does he say that salvation is based on?

REFLECTION

Through both the Day of Pentecost events (for Jews) and the conversion of Cornelius and family (for Gentiles), God shows his salvation is for all peoples on earth.

We need to be led by the direction of the Holy Spirit to help people find and enter the Kingdom of God. The wickedness of sin has raised to a climax of reaching God's anger. Therefore we need to go with the message of salvation to them.

People are only saved where the Holy Spirit is truly at work. But the Holy spirit is only happy to work where Christ is glorified and lifted up.

STUDY 6 - RECOGNISING AND DEALING WITH THE ENEMY OF THE HOLY SPIRIT

Ever since the Christian church started Christians have suffered for their faith. Many have been put to death because they were known to be believers of the Lord Jesus Christ. In many parts of the world today Christian are still being persecuted and killed because they believe in Christ and want to follow Him.

Christ warned that this would happen so we should not be surprised.

📖 Read John 16:33; 15:18-25

We should expect to suffer persecution because we believe in Jesus. What are some of the ways we can suffer or be persecuted?

✎

The Gospels show many examples of where evil spirits took control of people before Jesus cast them out.

📖 Read Mark 9:14-29 (see also Matthew 17:14-19, Luke 9:37-45)

Did the boy's parents do anything wrong to cause the evil spirits to control the boy?

✎

No. The world in which we live is spoilt by sin. This boy represents a mad earth today. We are fighting between good and evil every day because Satan wants to win over Jesus for our lives.

LIFE IN THE SPIRIT

📖 Read Ephesians 6:12-18
Who is our real enemy?
✎

How can we fight him?
✎

In today's world of fighting people use high powered guns and even send missiles to destroy hundreds of lives within a few minutes.
We know Satan is our enemy.

📖 Read 2 Corinthians 10:4-6
What does this verse say?
✎

When we use divine power what does that power do?
✎
Vs 4

Vs 5a

Vs 5b

Vs 6

📖 Read Ephesians 6:10-12
Whom are we fighting with?
✎

Who is our war is against?

✎

Who is referred to by 'flesh and blood'?

✎

Who is <u>not</u> our real enemy?

✎

📖 Read Ephesians 6:13-18

We can stand against Satan and demons only in the armour provided by God.

Name the armour God provides in the chart below:
✎

Name of Armour	How to use it	Its purpose

📖 Read 1 Peter 5:8
What is the main goal of Satan and his evil spirits?
✎

Satan does not care whether we are weak or strong Christians. He attacks all.

📖 Read Mark 9:17-22
What had the evil spirit done to the boy in the past? Vs 17
✎

What does the evil spirit do to the boy now? vs 18
✎

What is the final work of the evil spirit to the boy? Vs22
✎

What is the evil spirit's response when he sees Jesus? Vs 20
✎

Satan hates what is good in a Christian and he uses many different techniques to try to trick us.

📖 Read Matthew 2:16
What does this verse teach us?
✎

📖 Read Job 1:18, 19, 20-22

What was Job's response when Satan's first attack was against his possessions?

✎

📖 Read 2 Corinthians 11:13-15

What is Satan's masterful deception?

✎

📖 Read Revelation 12:7-11

What does this verse say about the fate of the "accuser of the brothers"?

✎

What are Satans's activities against people?

✎

What are the believer's defence against Satan? Vs 11

✎

Position of Victory

Our position in Christ means we stand before God.
What do these verses say about our position of victory?

📖 Romans 8:1

✎

📖 Colossians 2:9-10, 15
✍

📖 2 Corinthians 2:14
✍

📖 Hebrews 2:14-15
✍

📖 Ephesians 1:21-22
✍

📖 Ephesians 2:6
✍

What are some of the traditional ways in our culture that brings victory from our enemies? List at least five. ✍

1.

2.

3.

4.

5.

REFLECTION

We must face the facts as they are. As Satan is real, demons are real and our battle is real. We can expect their evil influences to increase in the world and in the church.

What defences do Christians have and what direction should they take?

✍

Three important words – RECALL, RESIST, RELY
      RECALL the Word of God
      RESIST the enemy
      RELY on God's armour

STUDY 7 - THE FRUIT OF A FALSE SPIRIT

During a time of revival and spiritual blessing in the church, some men and women unfortunately try to make things happen by themselves and then try to control everything. There maybe a spirit of pretense, or they try to copy others. This has led people to cause division and confusion within the church. It has caused some people to be mentally affected and say it happened because of revival.

Example – It was back in 1987 when a village near Balimo was swept up by spiritual awakening. People flooded into the church each evening as the bell rang. Those who gathered were in a high spirit of worship. One day it happened that a women was controlled by an evil spirit and was led to the graveyards. In a few days she was totally controlled by evil spirits, it was very hard to control her. Now to this day she is on the streets of Balimo. There was no discerning of the spirit when it came down on that woman.

How can we help prevent a situation like this happening in the church?

The word "REVIVAL" is made up of two words.
> **RE** means "again" or "bring back"
> **VIVAL** means "life"

So revival is to bring back to life again.

Read Titus 3:5
What can we experience when we are saved?

What does the Holy Spirit do?

The Holy Spirit uses his power to bring back believers to spiritual life when the church or individuals in it are weak.

Religion without Christ destroys people.

 Read Matthew 12:38-45

This story shows a person who has had a spiritual experience and has cleaned up their life. But he did not put anything good in its rightful place. He put wrong things into his life and it became worse than before. His life was destroyed with wrong things as evil sporiots took over.

 Read again Matthew 12:38-39

In our culture what are some signs and miracles that people are looking for?

What does it mean to be a believer when you are looking for signs and miracles?

Vs 43-45 What is the end result of those who practice following false spirits?

Can we identify and define that practice of following false spirits in our own culture and community?

False Religion without Christ destroys itself

There are many 'churches' coming up that look 'Christian' but remember Satan is like an angel of light.

 Read 2 Corinthians 11:14-15

How would you address this verse to a person who has listened to the deception of Satan's lies and believed lies as truth?

What will be their end result?

 Read Galatians 6:7,8

Who am I pleasing?

What is meant by sinful nature?

What happens to the one who pleases the Holy Spirit?

Read 2 Peter 2:1, 15

Where have you seen false teachers among us today?

✎

Do they truly know the sovereign act of God for their own salvation? If 'No" what ways can we help them?

✎

God warned people in the Old Testament that if they turned away from Him they could even suffer madness (Deuteronomy 28:28).

 Read Luke 15:11-31

What does this story of a young man teach us about living in rejection of our Heavenly Father?

✎

REFLECTION

 Read Proverbs 14:12

Test your religious experiences to make sure they are from God's Holy Spirit through Christ's mercy. Following false spirits will lead to death.

STUDY 8 - TESTING THE SPIRITS

In the world we live in today we are faced with all kinds of spiritual beings. Some claim to be harmful, some claim to be protective, some heal. However among all these there is only one good spirit that God has promised to send through Jesus. (John 14:15-17, 20)

Read 1 John 4:1-6

Apparently some of John's readers were led astray by all kinds of teachings. In our culture today what kind of teachings have come to drive people out of the church or to other religious groups or churches?

In vs 1, what are we told to do?

In vs 2, what must a true teacher openly confess about the incarnation of Christ?

What kind of teachers do we have in our church and those around us?

What is their message about Christ?

Tests to see if it is the work of the Holy Spirit

Test 1

📖 Read 1 John 4:2, 3, 15

The Holy Spirit will always give glory to _____

📖 John 16:14-15
Where does this glory come from?

Test 2

The Holy Spirit will always work against the world and the kingdom of Satan

📖 Read 1 John 3:8, 1 John 4:4, 5

A true Christian thinks a lot about _____ with God (1 John 2:15-17).

A true Christian works to destroy ____ in his own life (Romans 8:13).

Why are many Christians happy with what they have at present and are not looking forward for eternity with God?
✍

Test 3

The Holy Spirit will always give great respect to God's word, the Bible.
 Read 1 John 4:6a

Scripture is the foundation of the church (Ephesians 2:20).
Scripture is the _____ of the Spirit (Ephesians 6:17).

The word of God (Bible) is the authority of all our ministry and all our attacks on the devil and of his schemes.

 In John 14:15 Jesus said "If you love me, you will obey what I command".
The word of God affects every part of our lives not just one or two areas of life.

Test 4

The Holy Spirit will always lead to a spirit of truth (speaking truth not lies).

 Read 1 John 4:6b

This will give us a true picture about who we ourselves are (1 John 1:8)
The Holy Spirit help us to understand that telling lies and listening to lies is the work of Satan (John 8:44-47)

Test 5

The fruit of the Holy Spirit is always love for God and love for other people.
 Read 1 John 4:7-21
This verse makes us think:

Do we love our brothers?
✍

Are we keeping a record of past sins? 1 John 2:9, 10
✍

Are we true believers? 1 John 3:14
✍

Are we tricking or deceiving ourselves? 1 John 4:20,21
✍

Are we humble Christians? John 21;15-19
✍

There can be false love. Thieves and evil people love and protect each other. False teachers love each other and meet, help and support others.

Do you have some examples of these people in your community?
✍

However, true Christians live together, show love for God, love each other and love their enemies. What do these verses tell us about this?

📖 Matthew 5:43-44,

📖 Luke 6:27, 36,

📖 Romans 12:19-20,

📖 Proverbs 25:21

REFLECTION

Use the 5 tests of the spirits in this study to check what is happening in your church and your life today.
How do you rate yourself?

It is easy to become proud and to criticise others for what they are doing or not doing.

📖 Look at John 21:15-19 and put yourself in the place of Peter.
Look carefully at what is happening in the church and test the experience to see whether it comes from God or not.
When it is from God then support it. If it is not from God, do not support it.

Some thoughts to bear in mind:
- Do not do what everyone else is doing, turn away from it if it is not good or supported by the Bible.
- Pray for God's help.
- Show people where they are wrong from God's Word the Bible.
- Show the love of Christ by your own way of living in obedience to Jesus through the Holy Spirit.
- Keep praying for true revival.

Bibliography

Dickson, Fred C, *Angels, Elect and Evil,* Chicago Moody Bible Institute, 1975.

McGee, Vernon J, *Thru the Bible Radio,* Pasadena Thomas Nelson Publisher, 1983

Prince, Derek, *Directions For Christian Living,* London, Christian Focus Publication Ltd, 1986

Ryrie, C Charles, *The Holy Spirit,* Chicago, Moody Bible Institute, 1965

Walvoord, F John, Zuck, B Roy, *Bible Knowledge Commentary,* Colorado Zonderan Publishing House, 1983.

NOTES:

www.ingramcontent.com/pod-product-compliance
Lightning Source LLC
Chambersburg PA
CBHW050321010526
44107CB00055B/2349